ABDO
Publishing Company

Get Rest

A Buddy Book by **Sarah Tieck**

VISIT US AT
www.abdopublishing.com

Published by ABDO Publishing Company, PO Box 398166, Minneapolis, MN 55439.

Printed in the United States of America, North Mankato, Minnesota.
102011
012012
 PRINTED ON RECYCLED PAPER

Coordinating Series Editor: Rochelle Baltzer
Contributing Editors: Megan M. Gunderson, BreAnn Rumsch, Marcia Zappa
Graphic Design: Jenny Christensen
Cover Photograph: *Shutterstock*: Vladimir Nikitin.
Interior Photographs/Illustrations: *Eighth Street Studio* (p. 26); *Glow Images*: ©Sean Justice/ Corbis (p. 15); *iStockphoto*: ©iStockphoto.com/ApuuliWorld (p. 27), ©iStockphoto.com/ Auris (p. 21), ©iStockphoto.com/ChristopherBernard (p. 9), ©iStockphoto.com/laflor (pp. 5, 30), ©iStockphoto.com/monkeybusinessimages (p. 29), ©iStockphoto.com/ scanrail (p. 21), ©iStockphoto.com/seanfboggs (p. 23); *Photolibrary*: Age fotostock (pp. 7, 26), Doc-Stock (p. 11), Flirt Collection (p. 13), Glowimages RM (p. 21), Peter Arnold Images (p. 11); *Shutterstock*: Jaimie Duplass (p. 21), Andreas Gradin (p. 15), Kamira (p. 17), Crystal Kirk (p. 23), Rob Marmion (p. 25), Monkey Business Images (p. 19), Phase4Photography (p. 30), SergiyN (p. 27), Greggory James Van Raalte (p. 7).

Library of Congress Cataloging-in-Publication Data

Tieck, Sarah, 1976-
 Get rest / Sarah Tieck.
   p. cm. -- (Get healthy)
 ISBN 978-1-61783-233-8
 1. Rest--Juvenile literature. I. Title.
 RA785.T54 2012
 612.76--dc23
                          2011033059

Table of Contents

Healthy Living

Your body is amazing! It does thousands of things each day. It lets you yawn, stretch, and see. A healthy body helps you feel good and live well!

In order to be healthy, you must take care of your body. One way to do this is to get rest. So, let's learn more about sleep!

Getting enough rest helps your brain work its best. It also helps your body grow and heal.

Under the Covers

All humans and most animals need sleep to be healthy. People spend about one-third of their lives sleeping! Most elementary-age children need 9 to 12 hours of sleep each night.

Scientists aren't sure why we need sleep. But, they do know sleep keeps our bodies and minds working their best.

WORD OF MOUTH

Newborn human babies sleep about 16 hours each day!

Sloths can sleep 15 to 20 hours each day.

Giraffes only need about 20 minutes of sleep each day.

Getting Sleepy

How does your body know when it is time to sleep? Every person has a body clock. But, it isn't like a wall clock or a watch!

Your body clock lets you know when to sleep and when to wake up. It does this by sending out **chemicals**.

When this happens, your body gives you signs it is time to sleep. You may yawn. Your body may feel heavy. And, your eyes may feel like they want to close.

Narcolepsy (NAHR-kuh-lehp-see) is a sleep disorder. People who have it fall asleep suddenly without meaning to! Many have low levels of certain chemicals in their brains.

WORD OF MOUTH

Most people sleep at night and are awake during the day. Darkness helps your body know it is time to sleep. Light helps you wake up.

Stages of Sleep

People sleep in five stages that repeat several times each night. The first two stages are light. The second two are deep. The last stage is a special type of sleep called REM sleep.

When you first fall asleep, your eyes close. You might start to make sounds and movements. But, you don't know you are doing this. That is because you are not **conscious**.

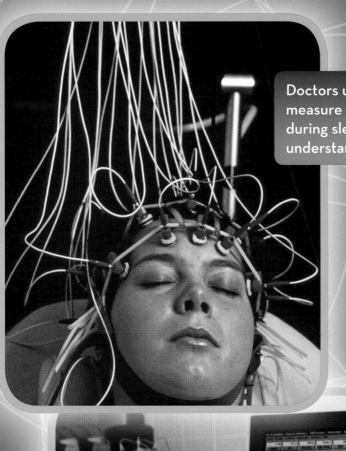

Doctors use an EEG machine to measure a person's brain activity during sleep. This helps them understand how a person sleeps.

An EEG machine records brain activity as waves. These waves look different during each stage of sleep.

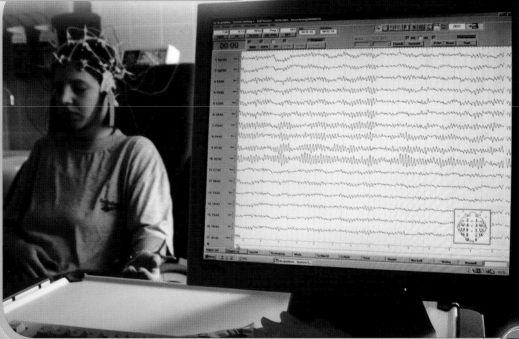

As you sleep, your heart rate and breathing slow down. Your **muscles** relax and your body **temperature** cools. Deep sleep recharges your body. Your brain also does important work, such as storing memories.

Sleep stages can be interrupted by loud noises. They might also be interrupted by changing light. If this happens, you may not feel as rested.

Create good sleep habits when you are young. This can help you sleep well throughout your life!

If your sleep is interrupted too often, you may have memory problems.

WORD OF MOUTH

Dream Time

Every person dreams. You may have four or five different dreams each night! You probably won't remember all of them. Still, many people believe dreams help you understand ideas and life events.

Doctors can use machines to see your brain's activity. But, only you can see your dreams.

WORD OF MOUTH

Flying is a common dream. Some people believe flying dreams are about freedom.

Writing in a dream diary can help you better understand your dreams.

Most dreams happen during REM sleep. *REM* stands for "rapid eye movement." In this stage, a person's eyes quickly move back and forth. This is a sign that he or she is probably dreaming.

If you wake up during REM sleep, you are likely to remember details of your dream.

Sleep Troubles

Sleep problems can have many causes. If you feel scared, it may be hard to sleep. Remember not to watch scary movies or read scary books before bedtime.

Sometimes, you simply do not feel tired at night. Many things can help correct this. Try not to eat a large meal or sugary food before bedtime. These can give you **energy**.

A bedtime **routine** can make it easier to fall asleep. Many people go to bed at the same time each night.

About 30 minutes before bedtime, try to do relaxing activities. Read, drink warm milk, or take a bath. Making these part of your routine tells your body it is time to sleep.

Drink this!

Not this.

Some foods, drinks, and activities help you sleep. Others can keep you awake.

Do this!

Not this.

Now and Later

Sleep helps your body stay healthy. Do you feel tired a lot or have trouble waking up for school? If so, you probably aren't getting enough rest.

When you are tired, you may have trouble paying attention. You might feel grumpy or forget things. And, you are more likely to catch sicknesses such as colds or the flu.

To wake up on time, set an alarm before you go to bed. Also, keep curtains open so morning sunlight can help you wake up!

Napping can help people catch up on missed sleep. But, napping late in the day can make it hard to sleep well at night.

Over time, not getting enough sleep can lead to other health problems. You could become **anxious** or **depressed**. You could also gain weight.

If you feel tired a lot, talk to your doctor. He or she can help you find a way to get more rest. Make good choices now to keep your body healthy for many years!

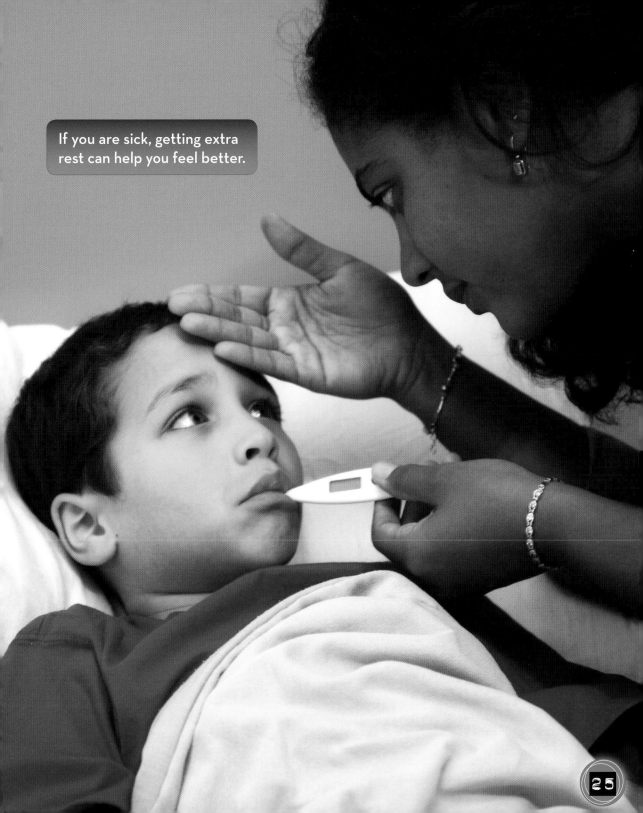

If you are sick, getting extra rest can help you feel better.

Brain Food

Sometimes I wake up late at night and have a hard time falling back asleep. What can I do?

Light and movement tell your body to wake up. So don't watch TV! Be sure your room is dark and stay in bed.

Why do I yawn when I'm tired?

Yawning usually means you are bored or sleepy. When you yawn, you open your mouth and breathe deeply. Many people believe this helps wake up your body and brain!

What causes snoring? Does it hurt?

Snoring happens because of the way people breathe when they sleep. Snoring doesn't hurt! Many times, people don't even know they are doing it.

Making Healthy Choices

Remember that sleep helps your body recharge and stay well! To fall asleep more easily, make a bedtime **routine**. When you choose to get rest, you make your body stronger and healthier.

Getting rest is just one part of a healthy life. Each positive choice you make will help you stay healthy!

How you feel during the day is often a result of how well you sleep.

HEALTHY BODY FILES

NIGHT TIME

✔ Some people feel more awake in the morning. Others have more energy at night.

✔ Sleepwalking is more common for children than adults. If you sleepwalk, going to bed earlier at night may help.

SCHOOL RULES

✔ Getting enough sleep can improve your memory. This can help you do well in school!

✔ The students with the best grades often get the most sleep.

BODY FUEL

✔ Most soda has caffeine. This chemical can keep you awake. Don't drink it close to bedtime!

Important Words

anxious (ANG-shuhs) afraid or nervous.

chemical (KEH-mih-kuhl) a substance that can cause reactions and changes.

conscious (KAHN-shuhs) awake and aware of one's surroundings.

depressed very sad.

energy (EH-nuhr-jee) the power or ability to do things.

muscle (MUH-suhl) body tissue, or layers of cells, that helps move the body.

routine (roo-TEEN) a group of actions that are done regularly.

temperature (TEHM-puhr-chur) the measured level of hot or cold.

Web Sites

To learn more about getting rest, visit ABDO Publishing Company online. Web sites about getting rest are featured on our Book Links page. These links are routinely monitored and updated to provide the most current information available.

www.abdopublishing.com

Index